ARIADNE AUF NAXOS

ARIADNE AUF NAXOS

IN FULL SCORE

RICHARD STRAUSS

DOVER PUBLICATIONS, INC.
NEW YORK

This Dover edition, first published in 1993,
is a republication of the original edition published by
Adolph Fürstner, Berlin, in 1916.
The title page and lists of characters and instruments in German
have been replaced by new English translations,
and a new English table of contents and glossary
of German musical terms have been added.

Manufactured in the United States of America.
Dover Publications, Inc.
31 East 2nd Street
Mineola, NY 11501

Library of Congress Cataloging-in-Publication Data

Strauss, Richard, 1864–1949.
Ariadne auf Naxos / Richard Strauss. — In full score.
1 score.
Libretto by Hugo von Hofmannsthal.
Reprint. Originally published: Berlin : A. Fürstner, 1916.
ISBN 0-486-27560-4
1. Operas—Scores.   I. Hofmannsthal, Hugo von, 1874—1929. II. Title.
M1500.S89A63   1993   93-12014
                                                CIP
                                                 M

CONTENTS

GLOSSARY OF GERMAN MUSICAL TERMS
in the Instrumental Part of the Score

aber	but	*früher*	earlier
alle	all	*ganze*	whole
allein	alone	*gedämpft*	muted
allmählich	gradually	*gedehnt*	lengthened
als	as, than	*gefühlvoll*	full of expression
auf	up, on	*gehend*	moving
ausdrucksvoll	expressively	*gelassen(er)*	(more) calmly
äusserst, aeusserst	extremely	*gemächlich(er)*	(more) leisurely
beginnen(d)	begin(ning)	*gemäßigter*	more moderately
behäbig	comfortably, comodo	*gemessen*	measured, moderately
bequem	comfortably, comodo	*gesanglich*	like a song
beruhigen	die down, lessen	*gesangvoll*	cantabile
beschwingt	quickly	*gestopft*	stopped
bewegt(er)	(more) agitatedly	*gesungen*	sung
Bewegung	movement, agitation	*get[eilt]*	divisi, divided
breit(er)	(more) broadly	*getragen*	sostenuto
Dämpfer	mute	*gewiss*	certain
dann	then	*gewöhnlich*	normal
dasselbe	the same	*gravitätisch*	solemnly
derb	coarsely	*Grazie*	grace
des	of the	*graziös*	graceful
deutlich	clearly	*groß*	big, large, great
die	the	*gut*	quite
Doppelgriff	double stop	*Hälfte*	half
doppelt so	twice as	*harpeggiert*	arpeggiated
drängend	pressing, stringendo	*heftig*	violently
dreifach	divisi in three	*heiter*	cheerfully
dreitaktig	in triple meter	*hervortretend*	prominently
durchaus	thoroughly	*hervortritt*	stands out
eilen	hurry	*Holzschlägel*	wooden stick
einfach	simple	*immer*	always, steadily
Einleitung	introduction	*innig*	heartfelt
enthusiastisch	with enthusiasm	*jedes*	each
erst	first	*kann*	can
etwas	somewhat	*klein*	small, bit
extatisch	ecstatically	*kurz*	short
feierlich	solemnly	*langsam*	slowly
ferne	distant	*laut*	loud
fest	firm	*lebhaft(er)*	(more) lively
Flatterzunge	flutter-tongue	*leicht*	lightly
fliessend(er)	(more) flowing	*leidenschaftlich*	passionately
folgen	follow	*leise*	softly
frech	saucy, brazen	*leuchtend*	glowingly
frisch	fresh, cheerful	*Marschtempo*	march tempo

Maß	measure, moderation
mäßig(er)	(more) moderately
mit	with
möglich	possible
nicht	not, don't
noch	still, yet
nur	only
offen	open
ohne	without
paar	couple
plötzlich	suddenly
plump	heavy
Pult	stand, desk
pultweise	by stand
rasch	quickly
rhythmisch	rhythmically
Rhythmus	rhythm
ruhig(er)	(more) calmly, peacefully
Saite	string
sanft	gently
Sänger	singer, tenor
schlagen	beat
schleppen	drag
Schluss	end
schnell(er)	fast(er)
schon	already
Schwammschlägel	soft sticks
schwärmerisch	ecstatically, effusively
schwer	heavily
schwungvoll	with impetus
seelenvoll	soulfully
sehr	very
seufzend	sighing
singend	singing
so daß	so that
Spieler	player
stark	strongly
stehend	standing
Steigerung	intensification, rise, increase
stets	constantly
Stimme	voice
streng	strictly
Strophe	strophe
stürmisch	stormily
süss	sweet(ly)
Takt	beat, bar
trotzdem	nevertheless
überschwenglich	extravagant
übrige	the rest, the others
viel	much
vierfach	divisi in four
voll	full
von hier aus	from here on
von jetzt ab	from now on
vorher	previously
vorig	previous
Vortrag	execution
weg	off
weich	tenderly
wenig	little
weniger	less
werden, werdend	become, becoming
wie	as
wieder	again
wiegend	swaying
zart	gently, softly
zärtlich	delicately
Zeitmaß	tempo
ziemlich	rather, quite
zögernd	hesitantly
zurückkehrend	returning
zurücklenkend	leading back
zusammen	together
zwei	two
zweite(r)	second

TO MAX REINHARDT
with Admiration and Gratitude
RICHARD STRAUSS   HUGO VON HOFMANNSTHAL

ARIADNE AUF NAXOS

OPERA IN ONE ACT
WITH A PROLOGUE BY
HUGO VON HOFMANNSTHAL

New Version

MUSIC BY

RICHARD STRAUSS
OPUS 60

CHARACTERS

Characters in the Prologue

The Majordomo [Der Haushofmeister]	Speaking Role
A Music Teacher [Ein Musiklehrer]	Baritone
The Composer [Der Komponist]	Soprano
The Tenor (Bacchus) [Der Tenor]	Tenor
An Officer [Ein Offizier]	Tenor
A Dancing Master [Ein Tanzmeister]	Tenor
A Wigmaker [Ein Perückenmacher]	High Bass
A Servant [Ein Lakai]	Bass
Zerbinetta	High Soprano
Primadonna (Ariadne)	Soprano
Harlequin [Harlekin]	Baritone
Scaramuccio	Tenor
Truffaldin	Bass
Brighella	High Tenor

Characters in the Opera

Ariadne	Soprano
Bacchus	Tenor
Naiad [Najade]	High Soprano
Dryad [Dryade]	Alto
Echo	Soprano
As the Intermezzo:	
Zerbinetta	High Soprano
Harlequin [Harlekin]	Baritone
Scaramuccio	Tenor
Truffaldin	Bass
Brighella	High Tenor

INSTRUMENTATION

2 Flutes [Flöten] alternating on Piccolos [kleine Flöten]

2 Oboes [Hoboen]

2 Clarinets (A, B♭) [Klarinetten (A, B)]

   Bass Clarinet (A) [Baß-Klarinette (A)]

2 Bassoons [Fagotte]

2 Horns (F, E♭, E, D, B♭) [Hörner (F, Es, E, D, B)]

   Trumpet (C, B♭, D, E) [Trompete (C, B, D, E)]

   Trombone [Posaune]

6 Violins [Violinen]

4 Violas [Bratschen]

4 Cellos [Celli]

2 Basses [(Kontra)bässe]

   Piano [Klavier]

2 Harps [(amerikanische) Harfen]

   Harmonium

   Celesta

   Timpani [Pauke(n)]

   Glockenspiel

   Tambourine [Tamburin]

   Triangle [Triangel]   } for 3 players

   Cymbals [Becken]

   Snare Drums [kleine Trommel]

   Bass Drum [große Trommel]

Vorspiel.

(Ein tiefer, kaum möblierter und dürftig erleuchteter Raum im Hause eines großen Herrn. Links und rechts je 2 Türen. In der Mitte ein runder Tisch. Tief im Hintergrunde sieht man Zurichtungen zu einem Haustheater. Tapezierer und Hausarbeiter haben einen Prospekt aufgerichtet, dessen Rückseite sichtbar ist. Zwischen diesem Teil der Bühne und dem vorderen Raum läuft ein offener Gang querüber.)

etwas lebhafter

12

Haushofmeister: Zuvörderst diese, darnach das für punkt neun Uhr anbefohlene Feuerwerk und zwischen beiden die eingeschobene Opera buffa. Womit ich die Ehre habe mich zu empfehlen.

(geht ab)

(Ein junger Lakai führt einen Offizier herein, dem er voran leuchtet)

Musiklehrer: roische Oper: A-ri-ad-ne? Wie soll ich das meinem Schüler beibringen? (ab nach der andern Seite)

12 etwas lebhafter

Lakai: (horcht) Hier finden Eure Gnaden die Mamsell Zerbi - net-ta. Sie ist bei der Toilette. Ich werde anklopfen! (klopft an die Tür rechts vorn)

etwas ruhiger

E-sels-kerl, läßt mich al - lein hier vor der Tür ___ hier vor der Tür mich stehn und geht.

(I. ohne Dämpfer) pizz.
arco
(II. mit Dämpfer)
(mit Dämpfer) pizz.
arco
pizz.
(mit Dämpfer) pizz.
arco
pizz.

(Seine Miene geht vom Zorn zum Ausdruck angestrengten Nachdenkens über)

Solo

ohne D.
I.Pult
4 Br. m.D.
II.Pult
m.D.
2 Celli m.D.
II.Pult

(alle get.)

O ich möcht vie-les än-dern noch in zwölf-ter Stund ___ und heut wird meine O-per ___ O der E-sel!

(Dämpfer weg)
pizz.
(Dämpfer weg)
arco
(Dämpfer weg)

18

22

26

dieser Welt kann keine Melodie ih-re Schwingen re - - gen!   Und ge-ra-de frü-her ist mir ei-ne recht schö-

(mit verändertem Ton, ganz gemütlich)

- ne ein-ge-fal-len!   Ich ha-be mich ü-ber ei-nen fre-chen La-kai-en er-zürnt,   da ist sie mir auf-ge-blitzt

da wacht man auf, da ist man bei der Sa-che! Und wenn sie in ihren Ka - rossen sit-zen, wis - sen sie ü-berhaupt nichts mehr, _____

Ken-ner und vor-nehme Per-sonen im Hau - se eines reichen Mä-cens: A - riadne ist das Losungswort. Sie sind A-riadne, und

38

39

44

Tanzmeister: das. Die Oper enthält Län-gen __ ge-fähr- -liche Längen. Man läßt sie weg. Diese Leu-te wissen zu im-pro-vi-sie-ren,

Tanzmeister: fin-den sich in je- -de Si - tua - tion. Fra-gen Sie ihn, ob er sei-ne O-per lie-ber

Musiklehrer: Still, wenn er uns hört, be-geht er Selbst-mord.

47

52

68

74

nor, dann die 3 Nymphen nach rückwärts, wo die Bühne angenommen ist, dirigiert und kommt jetzt eilfertig nach vorne, die Primadonna abzuholen, die noch einmal in ihr Garderobenzimmer verschwunden war.

82

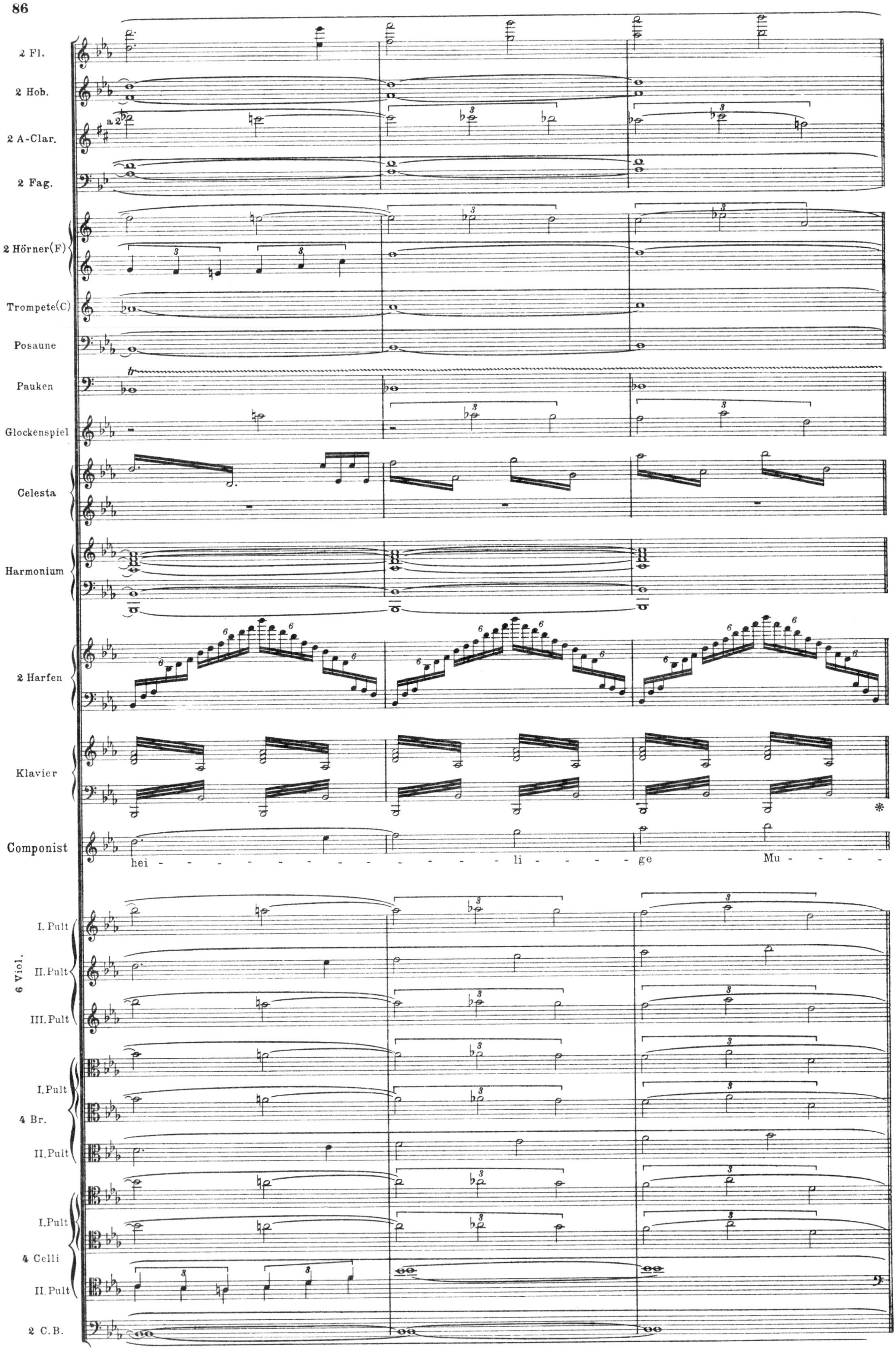
2 Fl.
2 Hob.
2 A-Clar.
a 2
2 Fag.
2 Hörner(F)
Trompete(C)
Posaune
Pauken
Glockenspiel
Celesta
Harmonium
2 Harfen
Klavier
Componist
hei - - - - li - - - - ge Mu - - - -
6 Viol.
I. Pult
II. Pult
III. Pult
4 Br.
I. Pult
II. Pult
4 Celli
I. Pult
II. Pult
2 C.B.

Zerbinetta erscheint rückwärts, mit einem frechen Pfiff ihre Partner auf die Bühne zu rufen.
Harlekin kommt eilfertig aus dem Zimmer rechts, läuft, seinen Gurt schnallend, auf die Bühne.
Scaramuccio kommt wie Harlekin, gleichfalls im Laufen seine Toilette beendend.

Wer hieß dich zerren mich— in diese Welt hinein? Laß mich erfrieren, verhungern, versteinen in der

88°

Ende des Vorspiels.

Oper.

Ouverture.

98

114

130

132

150

Recitativ und Arie.

172

180

Unterm Tanzen scheint **Zerbinetta** einen Schuh zu verlieren.

Sie läßt sich ihn von ihm anziehen,

Scaramuccio flink, erfaßt den Schuh und küßt ihn.

wobei sie sich auf **Truffaldin** stützt, der ihr von der andern Seite zu Füßen gefallen ist.

(Während die drei sich drehen, wirft sich **Zerbinetta** rückwärts **Harlekin** in die Arme und eilt mit ihm zu verschwinden)

168

194

200

227

234

Bacchus: hen! Cir - ce, du hast mir fast nichts ge - tan?

nächtli - chem Ent - zü - cken vor - aus _____ den schwa - - chen Sinn!

Ich weiß   nicht, was du re-dest.   Ist es, Herr, daß du mich prüfen willst? Mein Sinn ist wirr von vielem

260

266

dei-nes Man - tels der Mut - ter Au - ge auf mich her? Ist so dein Schattenland! al-so ge-seg - net?so un - - be-

319

284

Zerbinetta tritt aus der Kulisse,
weist mit dem Fächer über die Schulter auf **Bacchus** und **Ariadne**.

296

Zerbinetta, Harlekin, Scaramuccio, Truffaldin
und Brighella, desgleichen Najade, Echo, Dryade
haben von allen Seiten die Bühne betreten, zuerst ver-
halten sie sich horchend still.

Und e - - her sterben die e - - wi-gen Ster-ne, eh denn du _____ stürbest aus mei - - nem

THE END

Dover Orchestral Scores

THE SIX BRANDENBURG CONCERTOS AND THE FOUR ORCHESTRAL SUITES IN FULL SCORE, Johann Sebastian Bach. Complete standard Bach-Gesellschaft editions in large, clear format. Study score. 273pp. 9 × 12. 23376-6 Pa. **$10.95**

COMPLETE CONCERTI FOR SOLO KEYBOARD AND ORCHESTRA IN FULL SCORE, Johann Sebastian Bach. Bach's seven complete concerti for solo keyboard and orchestra in full score from the authoritative Bach-Gesellschaft edition. 206pp. 9 × 12. 24929-8 Pa. **$9.95**

THE THREE VIOLIN CONCERTI IN FULL SCORE, Johann Sebastian Bach. Concerto in A Minor, BWV 1041; Concerto in E Major, BWV 1042; and Concerto for Two Violins in D Minor, BWV 1043. Bach-Gesellschaft edition. 64pp. 9⅜ × 12¼. 25124-1 Pa. **$5.95**

GREAT ORGAN CONCERTI, OPP. 4 & 7, IN FULL SCORE, George Frideric Handel. 12 organ concerti composed by great Baroque master are reproduced in full score from the *Deutsche Handelgesellschaft* edition. 138pp. 9⅜ × 12¼. 24462-8 Pa. **$7.95**

COMPLETE CONCERTI GROSSI IN FULL SCORE, George Frideric Handel. Monumental Opus 6 Concerti Grossi, Opus 3 and "Alexander's Feast" Concerti Grossi—19 in all—reproduced from most authoritative edition. 258pp. 9⅜ × 12¼. 24187-4 Pa. **$11.95**

COMPLETE CONCERTI GROSSI IN FULL SCORE, Arcangelo Corelli. All 12 concerti in the famous late nineteenth-century edition prepared by violinist Joseph Joachim and musicologist Friedrich Chrysander. 240pp. 8⅜ × 11¼. 25606-5 Pa. **$11.95**

WATER MUSIC AND MUSIC FOR THE ROYAL FIREWORKS IN FULL SCORE, George Frideric Handel. Full scores of two of the most popular Baroque orchestral works performed today—reprinted from definitive Deutsche Handelgesellschaft edition. Total of 96pp. 8⅝ × 11. 25070-9 Pa. **$5.95**

LATER SYMPHONIES, Wolfgang A. Mozart. Full orchestral scores to last symphonies (Nos. 35-41) reproduced from definitive Breitkopf & Härtel Complete Works edition. Study score. 285pp. 9 × 12. 23052-X Pa. **$11.95**

17 DIVERTIMENTI FOR VARIOUS INSTRUMENTS, Wolfgang A. Mozart. Sparkling pieces of great vitality and brilliance from 1771-1779; consecutively numbered from 1 to 17. Reproduced from definitive Breitkopf & Härtel Complete Works edition. Study score. 241pp. 9⅜ × 12¼. 23862-8 Pa. **$11.95**

PIANO CONCERTOS NOS. 11-16 IN FULL SCORE, Wolfgang Amadeus Mozart. Authoritative Breitkopf & Härtel edition of six staples of the concerto repertoire, including Mozart's cadenzas for Nos. 12-16. 256pp. 9⅜ × 12¼. 25468-2 Pa. **$11.95**

PIANO CONCERTOS NOS. 17-22, Wolfgang Amadeus Mozart. Six complete piano concertos in full score, with Mozart's own cadenzas for Nos. 17-19. Breitkopf & Härtel edition. Study score. 370pp. 9⅜ × 12¼. 23599-8 Pa. **$14.95**

PIANO CONCERTOS NOS. 23-27, Wolfgang Amadeus Mozart. Mozart's last five piano concertos in full score, plus cadenzas for Nos. 23 and 27, and the Concert Rondo in D Major, K.382. Breitkopf & Härtel edition. Study score. 310pp. 9⅜ × 12¼. 23600-5 Pa. **$11.95**

CONCERTI FOR WIND INSTRUMENTS IN FULL SCORE, Wolfgang Amadeus Mozart. Exceptional volume contains ten pieces for orchestra and wind instruments and includes some of Mozart's finest, most popular music. 272pp. 9⅜ × 12¼. 25228-0 Pa. **$12.95**

THE VIOLIN CONCERTI AND THE SINFONIA CONCERTANTE, K.364, IN FULL SCORE, Wolfgang Amadeus Mozart. All five violin concerti and famed double concerto reproduced from authoritative Breitkopf & Härtel Complete Works Edition. 208pp. 9⅜ × 12¼. 25169-1 Pa. **$10.95**

SYMPHONIES 88-92 IN FULL SCORE: The Haydn Society Edition, Joseph Haydn. Full score of symphonies Nos. 88 through 92. Large, readable noteheads, ample margins for fingerings, etc., and extensive Editor's Commentary. 304pp. 9 × 12. (Available in U.S. only) 24445-8 Pa. **$13.95**

COMPLETE LONDON SYMPHONIES IN FULL SCORE, Series I and Series II, Joseph Haydn. Reproduced from the Eulenburg editions are Symphonies Nos. 93-98 (Series I) and Nos. 99-104 (Series II). 800pp. 8⅜ × 11¼. (Available in U.S. only) Series I 24982-4 Pa. **$14.95** Series II 24983-2 Pa. **$15.95**

FOUR SYMPHONIES IN FULL SCORE, Franz Schubert. Schubert's four most popular symphonies: No. 4 in C Minor ("Tragic"); No. 5 in B-flat Major; No. 8 in B Minor ("Unfinished"); and No. 9 in C Major ("Great"). Breitkopf & Härtel edition. Study score. 261pp. 9⅜ × 12¼. 23681-1 Pa. **$11.95**

GREAT OVERTURES IN FULL SCORE, Carl Maria von Weber. Overtures to *Oberon, Der Freischutz, Euryanthe* and *Preciosa* reprinted from auhoritative Breitkopf & Härtel editions. 112pp. 9 × 12. 25225-6 Pa. **$6.95**

SYMPHONIES NOS. 1, 2, 3, AND 4 IN FULL SCORE, Ludwig van Beethoven. Republication of H. Litolff edition. 272pp. 9 × 12. 26033-X Pa. **$10.95**

SYMPHONIES NOS. 5, 6 AND 7 IN FULL SCORE, Ludwig van Beethoven. Republication of the H. Litolff edition. 272pp. 9 × 12. 26034-8 Pa. **$10.95**

SYMPHONIES NOS. 8 AND 9 IN FULL SCORE, Ludwig van Beethoven. Republication of the H. Litolff edition. 256pp. 9 × 12. 26035-6 Pa. **$10.95**

SIX GREAT OVERTURES IN FULL SCORE, Ludwig van Beethoven. Six staples of the orchestral repertoire from authoritative Breitkopf & Härtel edition. *Leonore Overtures,* Nos. 1-3; Overtures to *Coriolanus, Egmont, Fidelio.* 288pp. 9 × 12. 24789-9 Pa. **$12.95**

COMPLETE PIANO CONCERTOS IN FULL SCORE, Ludwig van Beethoven. Complete scores of five great Beethoven piano concertos, with all cadenzas as he wrote them, reproduced from authoritative Breitkopf & Härtel edition. New table of contents. 384pp. 9⅜ × 12¼. 24563-2 Pa. **$14.95**

GREAT ROMANTIC VIOLIN CONCERTI IN FULL SCORE, Ludwig van Beethoven, Felix Mendelssohn and Peter Ilyitch Tchaikovsky. The Beethoven Op. 61, Mendelssohn, Op. 64 and Tchaikovsky, Op. 35 concertos reprinted from the Breitkopf & Härtel editions. 224pp. 9 × 12. 24989-1 Pa. **$10.95**

MAJOR ORCHESTRAL WORKS IN FULL SCORE, Felix Mendelssohn. Generally considered to be Mendelssohn's finest orchestral works, here in one volume are: the complete *Midsummer Night's Dream; Hebrides Overture; Calm Sea and Prosperous Voyage Overture;* Symphony No. 3 in A ("Scottish"); and Symphony No. 4 in A ("Italian"). Breitkopf & Härtel edition. Study score. 406pp. 9 × 12. 23184-4 Pa. **$15.95**

COMPLETE SYMPHONIES, Johannes Brahms. Full orchestral scores. No. 1 in C Minor, Op. 68; No. 2 in D Major, Op. 73; No. 3 in F Major, Op. 90; and No. 4 in E Minor, Op. 98. Reproduced from definitive Vienna Gesellschaft der Musikfreunde edition. Study score. 344pp. 9 × 12. 23053-8 Pa. **$13.95**

Available from your music dealer or write for **free** *Music Catalog to Dover Publications, Inc., Dept. MUBI, 31 East 2nd Street, Mineola, N.Y. 11501.*